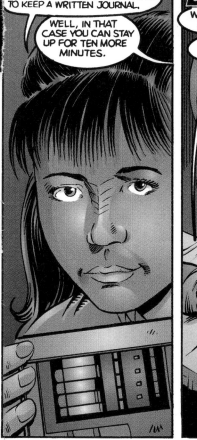

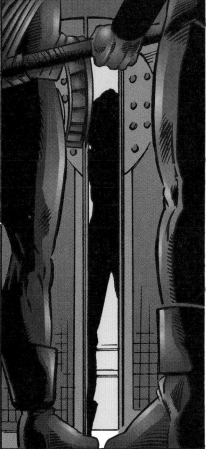

First published in Great Britain in 1995 by Boxtree Limited, Broadwall House, 21 Broadwall, London SE1 9PL. Published under exclusive license from Paramount Pictures, the trademark owner, STAR TREK: DEEP SPACE NINE art and text material © 1994 Paramount Pictures. All rights reserved. STAR TREK is a registered trademark of Paramount Pictures. STAR TREK: DEEP SPACE NINE is ™ ® © 1994 Paramount Pictures. All rights reserved. Any similarity to persons living or dead is purely coincidental. With the exception of artwork used for review purposes, none of the contents of this publication may be reprinted without the consent of the publisher. All rights reserved. 10 9 8 7 6 5 4 3 2 1. ISBN: 0 7522 0888 8. Except in the United States of America this book is sold subject to the condition that it shall not, by way of trade or otherwise, be lent, resold, hired out or otherwise circulated without the publisher's prior consent in any form of binding or cover than that in which it is published and without similar conditions including this condition being imposed upon a subsequent purchaser. Printed and bound in Great Britain by Cambus Litho, East Kilbride. A CIP catalogue entry for this book is available from the British Library.

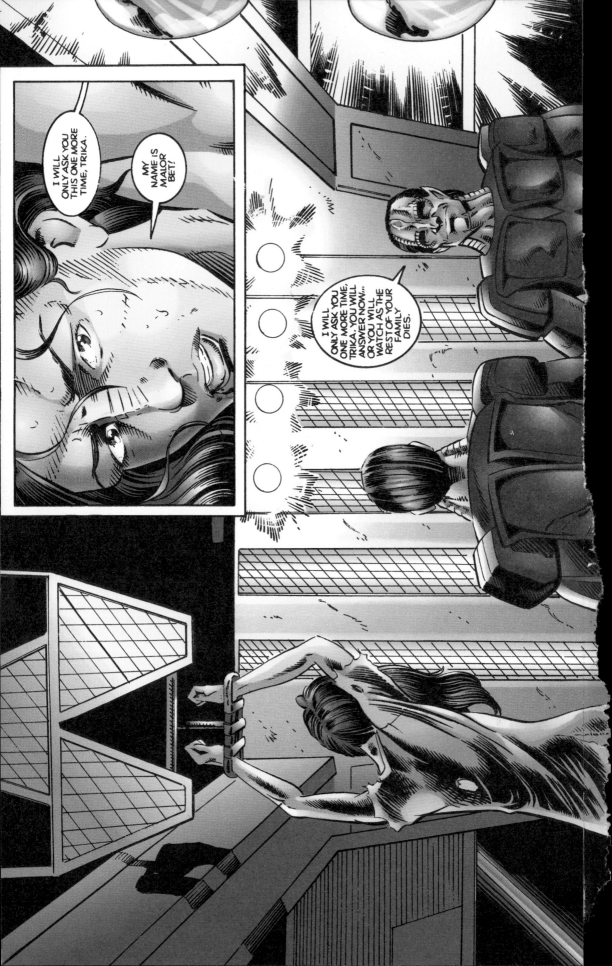

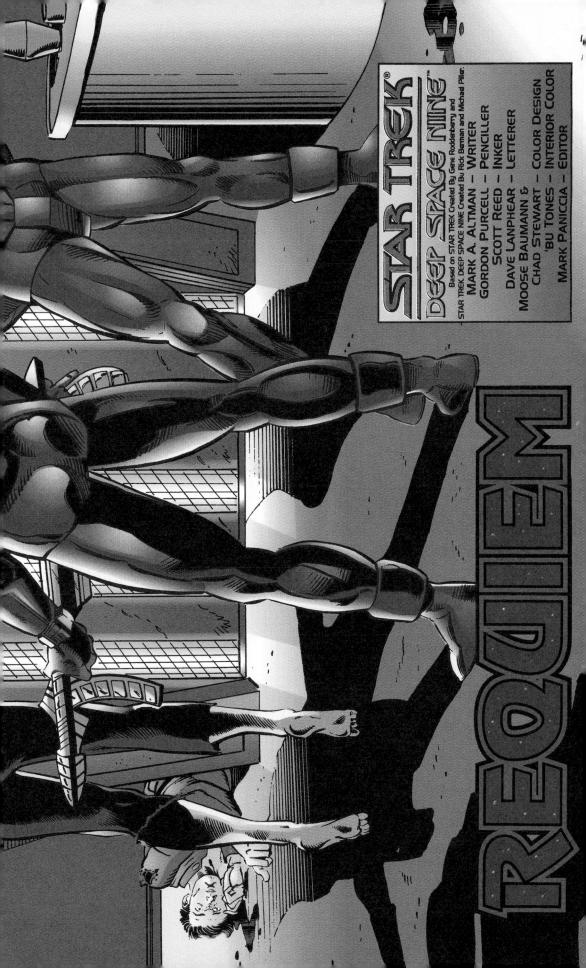

STAR TREK®
DEEP SPACE NINE™

Based on STAR TREK Created By Gene Roddenberry and
STAR TREK DEEP SPACE NINE Created By Rick Berman and Michael Piller.

MARK A. ALTMAN — WRITER
GORDON PURCELL — PENCILLER
SCOTT REED — INKER
DAVE LANPHEAR — LETTERER
MOOSE BAUMANN &
CHAD STEWART — COLOR DESIGN
BU TONES — INTERIOR COLOR
MARK PANICCIA — EDITOR

REQUIEM

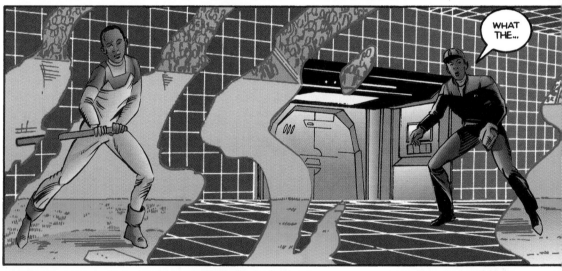

IT'S NOT LIKE YOU TO SECOND-GUESS YOURSELF. WHAT'S WRONG?

I'M PUTTING A LOT OF FAITH IN A CARDASSIAN.

I ASSUME YOU HAVE YOUR REASONS ...WHAT ARE THEY?

IT'S A LONG STORY.

I HAVE TIME. I'M NOT DUE IN STELLAR-CARTOGRAPHY UNTIL 1300.

DULATH USED TO BE CHIEF ENGINEER ON THIS STATION.

I KNOW THAT.

WHAT YOU DON'T KNOW IS THAT HE WAS REASSIGNED A YEAR BEFORE THE FEDERATION TOOK OVER DS9. WE SUSPECT IT WAS BE-CAUSE HE TRIED TO HAVE THE STATION SHUTDOWN BECAUSE OF HIS DISCOVERY OF THE CONTAMINATION FROM THE LEAKING REACTORS. HIS IMPACT STUDIES ABOUT THE EFFECT OF THE RADIOACTIVITY ON THE POPULATION EVEN-TUALLY LED TO THE CARDASSIANS SHUTTING DOWN FOUR OF THE STATION'S SIX REACTORS WHICH WERE LEAKING SODIUM...

...BUT THEY WEREN'T HAPPY ABOUT IT.

I WOULDN'T HAVE KNOWN ANYTHING ABOUT HIM MYSELF EXCEPT THAT HE'S A MEMBER OF THE CARDASSIAN SCIENTIFIC DELEGATION SCHEDULED TO ARRIVE NEXT MONTH TO STUDY THE WORMHOLE.

AND YOU HAD YOUR CARDASSIAN NEIGHBORS INVESTIGATED BEFORE ALLOWING THEM ON YOUR STATION.

SOMETHING LIKE THAT, OLD MAN.

IT'S FORTUNATE I KNEW ABOUT DULATH. I JUST HOPE IT WAS THE RIGHT DECISION.

WHAT AN UNEXPECTED DELIGHT, IF IT ISN'T MY FAVORITE BAJORAN MAJOR.

THERE WAS A LITTLE BAJORAN GIRL, SHE CAME TO YOU FOR FOOD DURING THE OCCUPATION, WHAT WAS HER NAME?

WHAT? PUT ME DOWN, YOU'RE HURTING ME.

SHE WAS HIDING FROM THE CARDASSIANS.

HOLD ON NOW, MAJOR.

SHE WAS THE DAUGHTER OF THE WOMAN THE CARDASSIANS CALLED TRIKA.

WHAT WAS HER NAME, QUARK!

I DON'T KNOW! THERE WERE SO MANY ORPHANS BACK THEN. TELL HER I DON'T KNOW O'BRIEN.

HER NAME WAS TI, MALOR TI.

WHAT? YOU KNEW HER?

I KNEW OF HER. HER MOTHER WAS THE HEAD OF THE BAJORAN RESISTANCE ABOARD THIS STATION.

SHE WAS EXECUTED.

KIRA TO SISKO.

YES MAJOR, WHAT IS IT?

CAN I SEE YOU COMMANDER.

WHERE?

HOLOSUITE 5.

WHAT CAN I DO FOR YOU AT THIS TIME OF NIGHT?

DAX TO SISKO.

ONE SECOND, MAJOR. GO AHEAD LIEUTENANT.

LATER...

ARE THE SEARCH TEAMS POSTED YET?

ALREADY SCOURING THE STATION, AS YOU REQUESTED.

IF YOU WERE A SCARED LITTLE *GIRL*, WHERE DO YOU THINK YOU WOULD HIDE?

I DON'T KNOW, MAYBE IN ONE OF THE ELECTRICAL CRAWLSPACES ALONG THE DOCKING PYLONS. WHY?

BECAUSE I WANTED TO KNOW WHERE *I* SHOULD BEGIN MY SEARCH.

YOU? WHY ODO?

BECAUSE YOU'RE MY FRIEND MAJOR.

AND YOU'RE THE *CLOSEST* PERSON I HAVE TO *FAMILY* THAT I KNOW OF IN THIS UNIVERSE -- AND I WANT TO *HELP* IF I CAN.

ANYWAY, I THINK I CAN MANAGE TO GET AROUND THIS STATION A LITTLE *BETTER* THAN OUR GREEN STARFLEET RECRUITS WHO GET LOST GOING BETWEEN DOCKING RINGS.

THANK YOU CONSTABLE.

CAN I JUST ASK YOU *WHY* THIS IS SO IMPORTANT TO YOU, MAJOR?

BECAUSE I WAS A SCARED LITTLE GIRL... ONCE.

"I REMEMBER ONE NIGHT WHEN I WAS ABOUT SEVEN YEARS OLD, I WOKE UP TO A LOUD EXPLOSION. I THOUGHT IT WAS THUNDER, IT WASN'T."

"IT WAS THE MIDDLE OF THE NIGHT AND MY ROOM SHOOK AND EXPLODED IN LIGHT."

"I WATCHED A BAJORAN FIGHTER INCINERATED AS DEBRIS FELL ACROSS THE CITY. I RAN TO MY PARENTS' ROOM, THEY WEREN'T THERE. I THOUGHT I'D NEVER SEE THEM AGAIN."

"I THOUGHT I WAS COMPLETELY ALONE."

"WHEN THEY CAME HOME THE NEXT MORNING, I FOUND OUT THEY WERE AT A SECRET MEETING OF THE RESISTANCE. THEY DIDN'T TELL ME WHERE THEY WERE GOING IN CASE THEY WERE CAUGHT, TO PROTECT ME. BUT THOSE 15 HOURS -- WHEN I THOUGHT THEY WERE DEAD, TAKEN BY THE CARDASSIAN POLICE -- OF ALL THE HORROR, BRUTALITY AND TORTURE I'VE EXPERIENCED, THOSE WERE THE WORST 15 HOURS OF MY LIFE."

AT LEAST *YOU* HAVE A PAST, MAJOR.

MEANWHILE...

WHAT WE'RE PROPOSING MAY SEEM UNORTHODOX COMMANDER, BUT I ASSURE YOU IT *SHOULD* WORK.

WHAT DO YOU ESTIMATE THE MARGIN OF ERROR TO BE, CHIEF?

CHIEF?

I THINK YOU BETTER COME UP HERE COMMANDER.

DO YOU KNOW WHERE WE ARE COMMANDER?

IF I REMEMBER MY ALTERNATIVE ENGINEERING CLASS AT THE ACADEMY, THIS CONTROLS THE REACTION CHAMBERS THROUGH WHICH THE POWER IS CHANNELLED IN CARDASSIAN REACTORS.

TOP MARKS, LOOK...

WHAT IS IT?

A PULSE WAVE CONVERTER RIGGED TO PICK UP RF EMISSIONS.

IN ENGLISH, CHIEF.

A BOMB. A VERY POWERFUL EXPLOSIVE DEVICE USED BY THE CARDASSIANS-- WHICH IS VIRTUALLY UNDETECTABLE TO TRICORDERS.

IF WE HAD *ACTIVATED* THIS REACTOR, DS9 *WOULD BE ASHES.*

IT'S A *GOOD THING* WE DON'T HAVE COMPUTER SYSTEMS ON-LINE YET. I WAS CHECKING EVERYTHING *MANUALLY.* THE COMPUTER *WOULDN'T* HAVE CAUGHT IT.

WHO HAD ACCESS TO THESE SYSTEMS...

"...BESIDES YOURSELF."

OPINIONS?

DULATH DID HAVE ACCESS TO THE REACTION CHAMBER, DID HE NOT CHIEF?

HE DID. THE ONLY WAY FOR US TO HAVE THE REACTOR UP AND RUNNING WAS TO WORK ON DIFFERENT SYSTEMS SEPARATELY.

BUT IF YOU'RE SAYING HE'S RESPONSIBLE FOR SABOTAGING THE REACTOR, I DISAGREE.

WHAT MAKES YOU THINK DULATH DIDN'T PLANT IT?

AN IRISHMAN'S BEST FRIEND, MY GUT.

YOU SAID YOURSELF THAT THOSE WERE THE SYSTEMS HE WAS RESPONSIBLE FOR REPAIRING.

AND YOU SAID YOU TRUSTED HIM COMMANDER.

I SAID IT WAS WORTH TRUSTING HIM. NOW I'M NOT SO SURE. IT IS A CARDASSIAN EXPLOSIVE DEVICE.

WE USED CARDASSIAN EXPLOSIVES AS WELL, IT COULD BE A BAJORAN.

WITH ACCESS TO A RESTRICTED AND SECURED AREA OF THE STATION?

I'VE GOTTEN TO KNOW DULATH, I DON'T BELIEVE HE'D DO SOMETHING LIKE THIS.

FROM WHAT YOU'VE SAID BENJAMIN, HE DOESN'T *SOUND* LIKE THE KIND OF CARDASSIAN WHO WOULD DESTROY HUNDREDS OF INNOCENT CIVILIANS.

I'M NOT *SAYING* HE IS GUILTY, I'M JUST *WONDERING* IF WE CAN AFFORD THE RISK.

WELL, I...

AS MUCH AS I'D LIKE TO BELIEVE YOU MR. O'BRIEN, THE EVIDENCE DOESN'T SUPPORT YOUR *GUT* INSTINCTS.

THE INFORMATION WE OBTAINED ON DULATH *COULD* BE AN ATTEMPT BY THE CARDASSIANS TO MANIPULATE US INTO EXPOSING OUR VITAL SYSTEMS.

CHIEF O'BRIEN, I THINK YOU BETTER TAKE A LOOK AT THIS.

THERE'S A MASSIVE ENERGY SURGE BUILDING IN THE CARBON REACTION CHAMBER OF REACTOR NUMBER TWO...

BROOOMM

WE'VE JUST LOST THE BACK-UP REACTOR...

ARE THERE *ANY* OBJECTIONS TO HAVING DULATH ASSIST MR. O'BRIEN?

WELL THEN, GO TO IT.

AYE, SIR.

OH, AND CHIEF, *GOOD LUCK.*

DO *YOU* REALLY TRUST HIM, MAJOR?

IF THE CHIEF TRUSTS HIM, THAT'S *GOOD* ENOUGH FOR ME.

YOU STILL SEEM WORRIED.

IT'S JUST THAT I NEVER THOUGHT I'D BE PUTTING MY FATE IN THE HANDS OF A CARDASSIAN.

SHORTLY...

I *WISH* WE HAD TIME FOR A FULL DIAGNOSTIC.

I *THOUGHT* YOU LIKED A *GOOD* CHALLENGE.

I DO... BUT NOT WHEN THE ENTIRE STATION'S *SURVIVAL* IS DEPENDING ON IT.

THE ENTIRE STATION IS DEPENDING ON THE FACT THAT YOU'RE RIGHT AND I'M *NOT* RESPONSIBLE FOR PLANTING THAT BOMB.

YOU *SHOULDN'T* TRUST ME, YOU KNOW. I AM A CARDASSIAN.

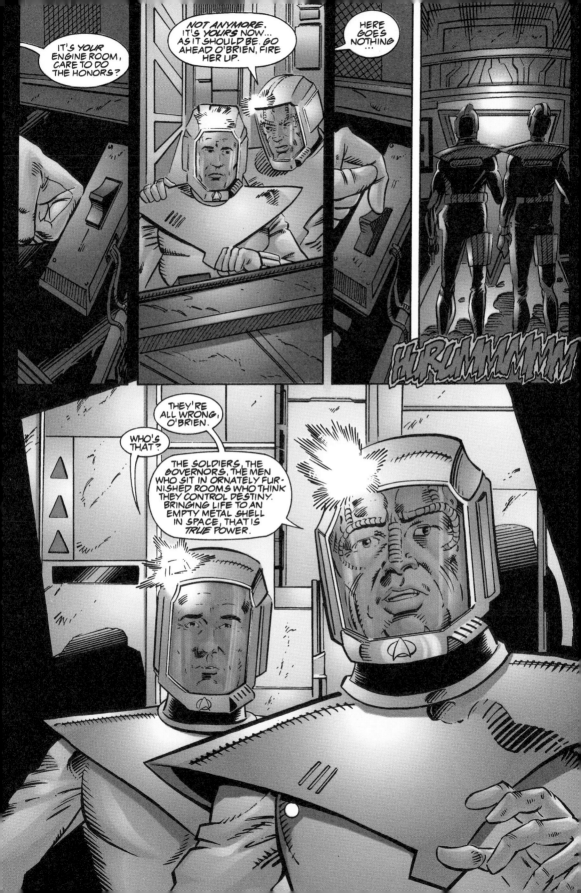

COMMANDER, THEY'VE ACTIVATED THE REACTOR. IT'S AT 5%...

10%.

25%.

50%.

75%.

90%.

95%.

NO, THERE'LL BE NO AUTOPSY. WE'LL BURY HER ON BAJOR... NEXT TO HER PARENTS.

AS YOU WISH MAJOR.

DID YOU FIND ANYTHING WITH HER, ANY BELONGINGS?

JUST THIS...

LATER...

BUZZZZ

COME.

CAN I TALK TO YOU FOR A SECOND COMMANDER?

OF COURSE, WHAT IS IT MAJOR?

"SHE SNUCK INTO THE ARMORY THROUGH THE VENTILATOR SHAFT, SET THE BOMB AND WAITED FOR THE CARDASSIANS TO BRING REACTOR #5 BACK ON-LINE."

"THEY NEVER DID BECAUSE OF THE RADIOACTIVE CONTAMINATION, THE RADIOACTIVITY THAT KILLED HER."

ARE YOU *SURE* YOU'RE GOING TO BE ALL RIGHT, MAJOR?

I DON'T KNOW.

SHORTLY...

I HAVE SO MANY QUESTIONS FOR YOU THAT YOU'LL NEVER BE ABLE TO ANSWER. WHAT DID YOU LIKE TO EAT? WHAT SONGS DID YOU LIKE YOUR PARENTS TO SING TO YOU? DID YOU THINK COL ZED WAS CUTE TOO?

HOW *DID* YOU LIVE WITH THE LONELINESS? THE SOLITUDE? *THOSE* ANSWERS, THEY AREN'T IN HERE.

I CAN'T *RECREATE* YOU TI, I CAN ONLY *REMEMBER* YOU AND WHAT YOU REPRESENT. I WON'T LET THEM *FORGET.*

BAJOR WILL ALWAYS REMEMBER THE NAME MALOR TI.

COMPUTER... DISCONTINUE AND DELETE PROGRAM.

CARDASSIAN SHIP GALVAR, YOU ARE CLEARED FOR DOCKING ON PYLON 3.

MY COMPATRIOTS HAVE ARRIVED TO TAKE ME BACK TO THE *BEAUTIFUL* DILITHIUM MINING PLATFORM ON WHICH I AM NOW POSTED ON ELYSSIA 3. HOW THOUGHTFUL.

I JUST WANT TO THANK YOU FOR *EVERYTHING* YOU'VE DONE FOR US, DULATH.

THERE'S JUST ONE MORE THING BEFORE YOU GO. *WHY?* WHY DID YOU COME BACK?

WHY? BECAUSE YOU ASKED.

THAT'S NOT AN ANSWER, DULATH. IT'S AN EVASION.

AH, MY FRIENDS HAVE ARRIVED.

I HOPE THE HUMANS HAVEN'T BEEN GIVING YOU *TOO* MUCH TROUBLE DULATH.

NO, BUT APPARENTLY *OUR* SOPHISTICATED TECHNICAL SYSTEMS HAVE BEEN GIVING THEM QUITE A BIT OF TROUBLE.

HAHAHAHA

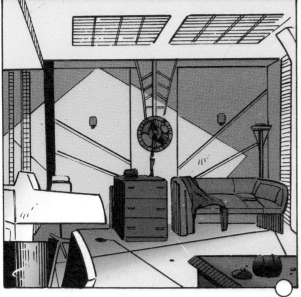

"Dear Diary, Today I lost a good friend..."

The End

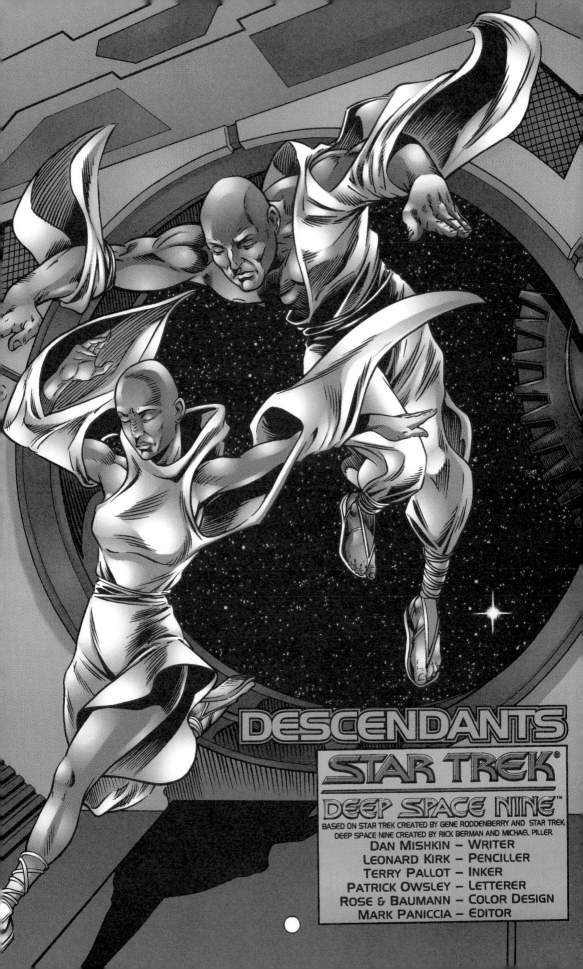

DESCENDANTS

STAR TREK®

DEEP SPACE NINE™

BASED ON STAR TREK CREATED BY GENE RODDENBERRY AND STAR TREK:
DEEP SPACE NINE CREATED BY RICK BERMAN AND MICHAEL PILLER.

DAN MISHKIN — WRITER
LEONARD KIRK — PENCILLER
TERRY PALLOT — INKER
PATRICK OWSLEY — LETTERER
ROSE & BAUMANN — COLOR DESIGN
MARK PANICCIA — EDITOR

COMMANDER. THE LEGENDS OF THE PROPHETS SAY THAT THEY FOUGHT A GREAT WAR AGAINST POWERFUL FOES...

...FOES WHO REPRESENTED EVIL AND DEATH AND DESTRUCTION.

DEVILS TO THEIR ANGELS, IS THAT IT?

I CANNOT SAY FOR CERTAIN, BENJAMIN SISKO.

BUT IF I UNDERSTAND YOUR REFERENCES CORRECTLY, I BELIEVE IT MAY BE SO.

I WONDER, COMMANDER. IF WE MIGHT HAVE THE FREEDOM TO ROAM YOUR STATION IN ITS ENTIRETY--

--PERHAPS WE WOULD FIND SPECIFIC EVIDENCE OF THOSE WHOSE PRESENCE WE FELT.

I SEE NO HARM IN THAT. ANY OBJECTIONS, MAJOR KIRA.

NOT ANYMORE, SIR.

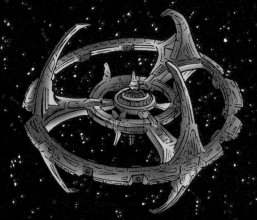

"WELL, IF NOTHING ELSE..."

"...IT CAUGHT THE WORMHOLE'S ATTENTION."